Manipula
Beginners

Learn The Simple Techniques And Discover Your Potential

Written By

Mark Panic

Table of Contents

INTRODUCTION

Thank you for purchasing this book!

The word manipulation is used primarily in our language with two senses, on the one hand, to refer in a general way to the handling that is carried out on various elements, utensils, which precisely require from those who employ them a finished knowledge and expertise. This is because they are objects that have in their functional structure an absolute consistency in the action they generate or perform when used.

And on the other hand, we use the term to designate that person or group, which using various characteristics that it has, such as the authority or power that it has in moral, social or political matters, uses it to get that person or group to not issue or express individual opinions, so that they do or not such or that thing.

That is, manipulation is what seeks to direct the opinion and thought of the other, nullifying their free will and their innate freedom, to orient it towards the end that best suits the manipulator.

Enjoy your reading!

Types of Manipulation

Before you can solve any problem, you must first identify it and find out what it is. The words manipulation and harassment are becoming more and more common. The media always talks about electoral manipulation, manipulation of capital, or manipulation of public opinion. The spotlight of the news, once focused on sexual harassment, is now focused on moral harassment.

Manipulation has many faces, sometimes very familiar. The buddy who invites himself unexpectedly (without worrying about the possible inconvenience) or someone who regularly borrows tools, books, or money without ever returning them to us are manipulators. The colleague who gets the project or the position that would typically have been given to us, the girlfriend who always ridicules what we do or finally, an individual with whom a conversation puts "our morale in the socks." Are these people inevitable? Are there people more sensitive than others to manipulation? Is it an evil that we have to endure by clenching our teeth, or can we do something to avoid manipulators and defend ourselves?

Before we can answer these questions, we must begin by knowing what manipulation is, what it is made of, and how it works. Starting from these solid bases, we will be able to discover the means and the tools to be implemented so as not to be manipulated anymore.

Basically, there are three types of manipulation that are distinguished from each other by the specific intent of the manipulator.

- In the first type of manipulation, the intention of the manipulator is always good, useful, or pleasant for the one who is the victim.

- In a second manipulative mode, the intent of the manipulator is egocentric. The manipulator turns the world around his personal interests, without worrying about the consequences for his victims.

- The intent of the manipulator, in the third kind of manipulation, is paranoid and always aims at a destructive and malicious purpose.

<u>Positive Manipulation (Type I)</u>

The intention of positive manipulation is consistently good, useful, or enjoyable. Even if it is not really manipulation in the sense that we usually hear it, it is essential to talk about it, if only to better perceive the other dubious types of manipulation that are hidden behind naive appearances.

Giving a gift or a pleasant surprise to someone is a type I manipulation, but offering an empty box to a child for his birthday and laughing loudly at his disappointment is not a type I manipulation even if the adult claims the opposite. This first type of manipulation (as its name suggests) always contains a positive intention; it's the opposite of blackmail. Even when a parent is pushing hard to get his child to wash his teeth regularly or when a nurse is giving a comforting speech with a syringe in her hand (do not be afraid, you will not feel anything), the intention remains good and aims in the direction of good, better, pleasant or useful. Sweet persuasion is a kind of positive manipulation.

A mother can persuade her child who is reluctant to work by saying: "If you finish your morning assignment, you will have all the afternoon to do what you like, otherwise you will spend the day unhappy." We can also manipulate someone by showing the positive aspects of something that displeases them. "Listen, I cannot go home on time because I have to stay in the office... I know it's boring, but it will allow me to go home earlier on Friday and have a better weekend."

Whether it's called bargaining, diplomacy, negotiation, mere advice, or persuasion, it's always about manipulation. But this corresponds to a type I manipulation because the intention starts from the heart and the manipulator seeks the good of the person who is the object of the manipulation.

If, on the other hand, you are made to believe that something is good for you when you know or feel the opposite, be certain that it is not a type I manipulation. Read on to stop letting yourself go!

Egocentric Manipulation (Type II)

The intention that guides the egocentric manipulator is the search for his own personal benefit. He thinks only of his interests, without worrying about the inconvenience, embarrassment, or discomfort that his behavior may cause others. The type II manipulator is trivial, cunning, deceitful, resourceful, and talkative. He is often guided by the lure of material gain, power, or fame; thinking only of himself, he always acts selfishly.

Type II manipulation is the kind we are subjected to when we are deceived, manipulated or trapped by someone who seeks to acquire something that he could not otherwise obtain.

Jean-Pierre, who had no particular qualifications, but who possessed a lot of charm and who knew how to speak, went door-to-door to sell encyclopedias. He was very successful because he had discovered that he was very convincing to the elderly who, trusting his good looks, signed the contract without knowing what they were engaging in. He was not worried about whether their low incomes would allow them to pay bills that amounted to more than a month's salary. The essential thing for him was to have contracts; that was his livelihood.

The type II manipulator is that friend who asks us for a service or money by making sure that we cannot refuse him. He is also the one who, to show his spirit, cracks jokes and laughs without knowing how to stop when it becomes offensive. He is also the employee who puts a spoke in the wheel of his colleagues to get a promotion in their place. He is the teacher who terrifies his class to prove his power, or he is the journalist who dramatizes a subject to be certain that his report will get airtime ahead of his competitors. None of these characters act maliciously. Basically, they do not want to hurt anyone. No, they simply focus on their personal interests without thinking or worrying too much about the consequences.

A lot of quarrels or separations are due to this type of manipulator. It is the "macho" husband who wants to show his authority and his independence by doing only what interests him, without taking into account the expectations of his wife. In trying to prove that he is the leader and that no one can command him, he does not see the upheavals that his behavior causes towards his companion. This man who thinks that he is so perfect will be surprised one day to see her go. Conversely, the woman who regularly contradicts or devalues her husband in public to show that she is not a submissive woman and that she has character turns out to be a manipulator.

Politicians who make promises and who, once elected, do not hold them, are type II manipulators, just like companies who relocate by dismissing their staff simply to increase profits. The latter think only of their interests, without worrying about future social disasters.

Marketing is fond of egocentric manipulations, as shown by the following example (an experiment conducted by researchers in social psychology).

When being offered a sample of pizza at the entrance to the supermarket, one in two agreed to taste it. But if the demonstrator touched their arm while making his proposal, two out of three accepted his offer.

Nobody has a rational explanation to explain this phenomenon, but to touch the arm of someone when making an offer is a small cause producing great effects, especially for the manipulator.

This last example shows us that some manipulations do not necessarily have harmful consequences. Unfortunately, most of our inconvenience comes from egocentric manipulations that we did not know how to prevent or that we could not resist.

Sylvie receives her old aunt who has asked to spend a few days at her home. But in accepting (or rather refraining from refusing this request), she could not imagine the nature of the visit. Starting the first evening, the aunt said to Sylvie: "Tomorrow we will start by visiting this exhibition which opens at 10 am, and then we will go eat in your usual restaurant. This way I'll see where you work and then you'll be able to use your coupons at restaurants. In the afternoon, we will go to the department stores and in the evening we will end up in a tea room because I love tea. You know, I have not been in town for a long time, and it's a great pleasure for me to spend a few days with you."

Sylvie tries to protest, to explain that she cannot be free so easily, but her aunt does not let her speak and explains to her that she feels so lonely since her husband's death. Sylvie, touched, does not know what to say and her aunt takes the opportunity to add: "Come on! By the way, what are we eating for dinner? You know, I usually do not eat much at night, but for the time I'm with you, we could enjoy it. I'll let you choose the restaurant, I'm not difficult and as long as it's not too noisy, everything suits me."

Whether they are small rogues, marketers, politicians, companies, little bosses, selfish colleagues or "macho" husbands, the type II manipulator acts primarily to satisfy his interests. He does not intend to harm anyone. Totally focused on what he wants, he does not see or refuses to see the real damage that his behavior generates. However, we can discuss their actions with them and change their minds by focusing on their intellectual honesty.

Malicious Manipulation (Type III)

With this third type, we enter the field of the sneaky. This conscious and deliberate attempt to destroy others is extremely dangerous. Indeed, if the intention of the first type of manipulator is positive and that of the second selfish, the intention of the third manipulator is destruction.

The latter does not want the good of anybody, and he does not necessarily seek his personal interest. His sole and main purpose is to destroy what threatens him or what seems to be intolerable or hateful. We can sum up the intention of this manipulator by saying that everything he undertakes is intended to kill you, to ruin what you do, or to destroy an aspect of your personality that does not suit him.

The Two Characteristics of Type III Manipulation

This manipulation is characterized by malevolent and perverse intent as well as concealment of his attacks.

A Malicious and Perverse Intention

When he harms someone, the malicious manipulator often claims the opposite and claims that he is acting for the good of his victim or for a just cause. Malicious intent often hides behind apparent honesty.

Michael is an educator and cares for handicapped children. One day, he receives the unpleasant surprise of seeing the police enter his class to ask him questions because his wife, a manipulator with whom he is undergoing a divorce, accused him of having incestuous relations with his little girls between 6 and 8 years old. He defends himself and tries to explain that he has done nothing. But, to get custody of the children, his wife picks up and uses everything he says to "push" him further.

She pretends to act in the interest of her children. The accusation was, of course, unfounded, but the case still lasted several years during which it was totally impossible for Michael to meet his daughters without the presence of a social worker. He spent all his savings, lost all his property, his house, his car, his furniture, and went into debt to pay a lawyer. Because of his wife's false accusation, he was forbidden to work with minors and he lost his job. After several years of counseling, totally ruined and completely "demolished" both morally and physically, he is finally identified as innocent. The damage is done, and his life is broken. The manipulator has won on all fronts.

Hiding the Attacks

The manipulator always manages to destroy his victims without being noticed by them. He destroys but conceals it from those he seeks to defeat. This type of manipulation is like a silent and faceless destruction for those who do not know or do not want to see it.

Laurie is a chef and has lunch every day at noon with Myrtille, a colleague and friend. They take advantage of these moments of relaxation to talk about things and also to exchange ideas or advice when they encounter particular difficulties. Gradually, Laurie is sidelined and her responsibilities melt like snow in the sun. After having regularly reproached her for baseless misconduct, her supervisor removes all of her supervisory responsibilities and assigns her to a position where she has no one to manage.

For a long time, she tried to understand what had happened to her. She often talked with Myrtille about what her boss was doing to her. She tried, but to no avail, to find an explanation and to uncover the reasons for her downfall. She felt guilty and lost confidence in herself. One day, finally, she noticed that her "friend" Myrtille was now handling her former duties and taking over from the projects she had initiated. Laurie realized, a little late, the origin of her misfortune.

The Manipulator

The manipulator is a person with excessive pride who does not respect the other person and tries to prevent them from living in their own way. His goal is to diminish, belittle, or even destroy his victims. To achieve his goal, he uses misinformation, lies, or slander.

For an attentive observer, it is evident that he sows the seeds of trouble around him and that he puts people against each other. He is an expert in moral harassment who rarely intervenes directly, preferring to push others to act in his place. He is a coward who makes his victims feel responsible for and guilty of what he does to them, and that allows him to continue to destroy all innocence.

One can hardly impress him, nor have a hold on him. He seems unassailable and unshakable; he knows everything. We would like to be able to defend ourselves and counter-attack, but as he terrorizes people, they do not succeed or do not dare. When they try something, it usually turns against them, thus seeming to prove their persecutor right.

He says he is honest and fair, acting for your good or for a good cause. This defense system implies that he will never recognize his wrongs. When he is caught, he regrets nothing; he does not apologize and feels no compassion for his victims. He is very often obsessed with the idea of being in danger. This threat is so real to him that it allows him to justify and legitimize his evil deeds. This is how people are led to kill and torture in the name of their faith, their convictions, or their anxieties. They can even be proud of it.

A Monster!

It is hard to imagine that human beings can be so mean and hateful. A normal, healthy person has great difficulty in conceiving that such destructive and harmful intentions can be fostered. It's just as foolish as imagining oneself killing, torturing, or raping. However, in the same way that there are murderers, executioners, or rapists, there are also malevolent beings that spread evil around them.

To think that such individuals do not exist in our environment or to believe that they will get bored and stop their destruction process to change their strategy is an illusion. Worse, this error of judgment strengthens the manipulator and makes him even more formidable for anyone who believes such nonsense.

Eleonore, 32, a senior executive in a big company, is regularly beaten by a jealous husband who wants to make her confess that she is cheating on him. She often wears sunglasses and appropriate clothing so that one notices the marks of the blows she has received. Like many battered women, she does not trust anyone, lest her husband attacks her children. And she loves her companion and does not want to leave him. Eleonore wishes to continue her life as a couple and family. Over time, the situation seems hopeless, and she eventually sinks into depression.

One of the most common results of this type of manipulation is the feeling of guilt that overwhelms the victim. By concealing what is going on and what she is going through, she becomes, in a way the accomplice of her executioner.

This manipulation is, in many ways, monstrous. It is difficult to denounce because of the feeling of guilt already mentioned. This is often the fate of children who have suffered incest or acts of pedophilia. To the victim, the feeling of guilt is generally imposed by the manipulator: "It's your fault, it's you who pushed me to do that." Guilt slowly makes its way into the victim's mind and leads her to believe that she deserves her suffering, and the manipulator is right to behave as he does or that he is acting in her best interest.

Who Is He?

He has an anonymous, everyday face. He can be the father of a family who keeps his wife and children under an iron fist. He crushes them under his tyrannical law; he prevents them from thinking and living for themselves or taking any initiative. At the same time, he says loudly that he is a responsible parent who thinks and acts only for the good of his family. This is the case of a man who managed to prevent, discreetly and repeatedly, the marriage of his daughter to boys who, according to him, were not good enough for her.

Traits of Manipulative People

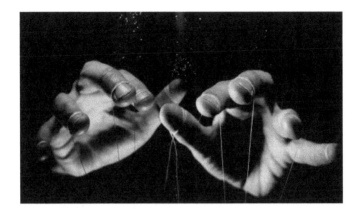

It's hard to think that people could deliberately try to control others. Everybody is taught from a young age that they should see the good in people, but then reality shows us that not everybody acts good and some people use people's weaknesses against them.

Manipulators view things in a different light. In fact, it's not too farfetched to say that a manipulative person actually understands people and life better than the rest of us. However, this ability is used to deceive others in order to get everything they want.

For a manipulator, they traverse the world like a chess board. They view others as expendable. On the outside, they act lovingly and caring, but this affection is only present in order to lure you in so that they can use you when needed.

Manipulators start observing others by learning about their own insecurities. They start looking into their emotional issues and then work to figure out why they have them. This information will then help them to observe others during the day. They watch people facial expressions, the words people use, and how they react towards things to learn about others. Things you say and don't say provides the manipulator a lot of insight.

The manipulator with then uses your personality and emotional state as a way to mold their self into your life. They will likely act very differently in front of different people. In front of you, they could act outgoing and fun loving, but when they are around another person, they play the victim. They enjoy coming up with their own story and character that plays right into their victim's life. This ensures that whatever they feel, their victim feels as well. This is because they create a strong bond with their victim. This bond could be created through kindness, friendship, guilt, victimization, authority, love, intimidation, and any other emotion that they choose to use. This allows the manipulator to control your thoughts so that you see the world the way that they want.

Tricking Others

Con artists like tricking others into giving them money or other "gifts." For a manipulator, manipulation is an art. They love it when their victim does or says exactly what the manipulator wanted them to. If a manipulator is trying to elicit fear into their victim, they will use shame, lying, bullying, and other tactics to trick the victim into feeling this way. Once the victim does start showing fear, it gives the manipulator a rush.

Manipulators keep score for their self whenever they succeed or don't. They are able to justify their own actions. To themselves, they may say things like:

- "If they choose to be so open, they can only expect others to use them. Why shouldn't I?"

- I am only using my talents in order to get what I want while also having fun. Everybody does that."

- "Everybody tries to manipulate others. I am just better at it."

These justifications work enough for them in order to continue manipulating others. This works only to further enhance their pleasure of tricking and controlling others. A manipulator's life is defined around their ability to force others to bend to their will.

They Want to Win

The manipulator calculated every move and action they make. They may not succeed in everything they do, but their intentions are always aimed towards victory. All a manipulator wants is for everybody around them to submit to them. It could be a romantic partner or a co-worker, but their goal is to find their vulnerabilities and use that against them. In fact, some are so good that they can use a person's strengths against them. For example, if a person is trying to be happy despite the negative things happening around them, the manipulator will show them a different picture of a happy life in order to get them to submit.

The techniques they choose to use will all depend on their purpose and victim. They can be the charmer or the bully depending on what they want to get from you. This is why, in romantic relationships, the manipulator can be a completely different person at different phases of the relationship. They will start out charming in order to trick somebody into loving them.

As the relationship progresses, they want to gain control over their partner's actions. This is when the intimidation, silent treatment, and blackmailing will start.

They have multiple masks and you never know which one they are going to be wearing on a day-to-day basis.

Great Communication Skills

Communication skills are the best weapon in a manipulators arsenal. Victims typically don't realize when the manipulator uses words that impact their mind, subconscious and conscious.

That said, a good communicator isn't always a manipulator, but you can guarantee a manipulator is a good communicator. Their skills include:

- Their ability for irony and sarcasm.

- They are confident when lying or arguing.

- They are great at vague facts and statements.

- They have great command over words.

If you try to confront a manipulator about something rude they said, they will turn the statement around to make it seem like a compliment. They are great at wrapping hurtful statements into compliments. For example, "I can't believe you rebuilt that engine. I didn't think you have any discernible skills."

Language is their way of shaking the ground of their victims, and then they use it to comfort them. At one point they can say great things, and then in a blink of an eye, they start insulting you. This is all to see how you react to different scenarios, which gives them the ability to read you better.

Their insults hurt, but their compliments will melt your heart. This is how they use communication to remove their self from any situation and create a new one.

They Look for Vulnerability

The manipulator views everybody as vulnerable. The only that is different between person to person is the extent of their vulnerability. People who are less vulnerable are harder to manipulate, while people who are more vulnerable are easy targets. Some manipulators like to watch less vulnerable people and try to attack them just for fun. However, they make sure they are in a safe place. Otherwise, they try to pick out the most vulnerable person and mess with their emotions to reach their end goal.

A person who has few friends would be an easier target than people who have several friends. They also look at a person's hopes, desires, happiness, career, confidence, and self-esteem to judge their vulnerability. When they have a choice, the most vulnerable personality will always be their target.

A firm-minded person won't even make them stop. They believe that everybody has hopes, so no matter how confident they are, they will target those hopes and turn them into vulnerabilities. The manipulator does sometimes lose, but a loss hurts them and they will continue to try until they reach victory.

They Trick Their Own Mind

In order to make their lies work and keep up with their charade, they have to make up stories. They work out every little detail of these stories and make sure that they are completely believable in their own mind. Even when they do lie, a part of the brain believes it to be the truth. This is how they can flawlessly remember those stories and keep up with their lies for years. They go through every possible question that could come up and they prepare for it. If anybody tries to question their logic, they will present them with a believable answer. Eventually, what started as a lie will turn into truths for the manipulator and their victim.

After a conversation with a manipulator, don't be surprised if you find out some, if not all, of what they said was a lie or half-truth.

Characteristics of Manipulators

- Self-centered

Every characteristic of a manipulator comes down to this point. Manipulators are self-centered people. They don't understand, nor do they care about other's mental state, life, thoughts, or emotions. The only interest they have in mind is their own. If they end up hurting somebody psychologically or physically, it is just collateral damage. People are expendable. This is their view of the world. No matter how charming, caring, or logical they may appear, they don't mean a bit of what they say. It is a specific formula of expressions, words, and emotions to help them manipulate situations and people.

- Jealousy

Manipulators would never admit it, but jealousy plays a big part in their mindset. For many, this is what drives their motivation to act people's vulnerabilities. Jealousy comes at them from several areas in their life because their main desire is to feel superior to everybody. This can cause them to feel jealous of their own friends, spouses, siblings, and parents. This jealousy sticks with them until they are able to gain control over the person they are jealous of. When they have a person's emotions in hand, they feel powerful and better than them.

If a manipulator feels jealous about the money a person has, they may target that person's loneliness. If a manipulator feels jealous about another person's looks, they may try to sabotage that person's relationship. Anything good in your life can cause a manipulator to feel jealous and they may decide to destroy that happiness.

A manipulator could also stay in your life with the simple purpose of exploiting your resources. They are only around you to enjoy the good things that you have earned. They will feel jealous about what you have, but they decide to make you share this with them instead of ruining it for you. For example, if you have created your business and it is successful, they may present their self as a helpful partner without actually helping your business or knowing anything about it. Similarly, if you are happy as an independent person, they may lure you into a relationship with them to share your life.

They want to feel and experience what you have, emotionally and physically.

- Indirect communication

While manipulators are great at communicating, they like using others to share what they want. They will make their self appear as straightforward, someone who says what they think. However, they plant seeds in the minds of others. You won't even know what they have done. They make you think you came up with the idea on your own so that when you do whatever it is, you get blamed for it.

They create their conversations using questions and will ask whether or not you agree. This ensures that they are always out of sight and you do their bidding. For example:

"Something needs to be done about Sharon. She keeps bad mouthing us to the others in the office."

"Really? I can't put up with this anymore. If she has something to say, she can say it to my face."

This is how a manipulator controls a conversation. They will plant the seed of some hidden message because they want you to do what they can't. Once you act on it, they stand back and say it was all you. "I only said what I thought because I was concerned."

By using other people as their messengers, manipulators can hide and have an escape in every situation. They write their scene and watch it play out. Nobody ever thinks that it was the manipulator tricking the others, and even if somebody were to discover this, manipulators will hold the others accountable for their actions. They make sure no matter how things turn out they will remain squeaky clean.

- Multiple personalities

Manipulators change to fit every scenario they find their self in. Multiple personalities live within everybody. However, not everyone will showcase or hide these different personalities in order to gain something, but the manipulator does. They mold their self to create a disguise for every victim, so if their goal is to scare their victim, they will never laugh or talk in a light manner in front of them. They stay in character at all times. You may think that your boss is a hard-ass around you, but around another person, they can be sugary sweet.

The ability to switch up their personalities makes them dangerous. In relationships, we often create an image of our partner, but what if the picture you have created is wrong? You see the perfect image of a partner, but they are actually cheating on you and getting by with it.

When they switch up their personalities, they focus on three things; feelings, behavior, and opinions. They choose to act in certain ways around certain people. They incorporate righteousness in the way they act to create trust. Manipulators have the ability to shake up their victim by switching up their behavior. If a wife is manipulative, they can choose to switch up her mood in order to keep her husband under control.

Manipulators also have the innate ability to debate for and against at the same time. They present their views in a vague manner so that nobody can hold them responsible. Switching sides gives them the chance to say what a victim wants to. If the manipulator is communicating with two different victims at the same time, they can easily get out of the situation using a vague statement, like, "You both have valid points. We need to keep an open mind in order to see everything."

Manipulators can be ruthless with feelings. They can observe how somebody feels and they use this to change their persona to act accordingly. If the victim does something bad and feels remorse, the manipulator will use this remorse in order to play the victim. When a person feels remorseful, they want to do something good to make up for their wrongdoing, so manipulators us this to get the victim to do what they want.

- Hidden insecurities

Behind all of their confidence are hidden insecurities. Observing feelings in others helps them to understand their own insecurities. However, they hide their insecurities and self-confidence very well. Every time they play the victim, there is a bit of truth in it. They use their insecurities to help mold their character in order to fool others.

These insecurities sometimes guide the manipulator towards vulnerable people. They look to gain attention in order to feel superior, but that is only possible if they can find somebody who is more vulnerable than they are. This starts their search for the right victim, and others will end up getting hurt in the process.

The manipulator's insecurities give them their obsessiveness towards achieving their goals. In a relationship, the insecure manipulator will find reasons to blame their significant other to hear them to apologize. Manipulators want to be followed. Some manipulators what praise and others want to control.

- Practical empathy

Empathy is having the ability to understand a feel the emotions of the others, but manipulators don't typically experience empathy. Manipulators use empathy when it suits them. They understand the feelings of others, but they don't share them. A manipulator is a lot like a robot. They are programmed to understand emotions, they just don't feel them.

If you sat down and talked about relationships with a manipulator, they will often divide them into wants, needs, and other practical parts. They can only explain love in logical terms. If a major celebrity were to marry a less famous celebrity, the manipulator would say the less famous one was trying to climb their way up the ladder.

Manipulators are able to see the need, hope, attraction, affection, rivalry, jealousy, and intrigue in relationships. They use these things to play people and ruin their relationship. They have the ability to encourage or discourage somebody to love or hate another. It all depends on what their big plans are.

- Motivator

Manipulators are great at motivating people others. Their power over communication gives them the ability to convey what the victim wants to hear. They are able us a person's emotional, practical, and caring abilities to motivate them to do things. For example, if a manipulator notices a person is insecure about their looks, they will praise their facial features.

They praise in subtle ways, though. Instead of coming out and say, "You look beautiful," they say, "Your eyes share your beauty." The way they approach the situation and the way they word their compliment will cause the victim to buy into their lies.

They can also motivate people using their bad feelings. If their victim is feeling down, the manipulator will motive the sadness to fulfill some purpose. They can do the same with jealousy, anger, hope, and fear.

The ability to motivate a person's feelings is a common aspect of all manipulators. They often use this to create a relationship with a person and to strengthen their bond with the victim.

- Self-confidence

A manipulative person doesn't have a shortage of confidence when it comes to their thoughts and actions. However, they can show and hide this confidence whenever they want. This gives them the ability to not take responsibility. This gives them the chance to shift the blame off onto somebody else. They control their puppets and then if it benefits them, they will come out as the confident person. They will even take responsibility if it suits their purpose.

- Don't consider personal space

Manipulators who are not aware of the fact that they are manipulators lack an understanding of their personal identity. But, manipulators who deliberately manipulate others don't care about personal space. A manipulator can attack every aspect of a person's life or only a single area.

If their manipulation is forceful, it will cause the victim to experience exhaustion. Intimidators, abusers, and other direct manipulators will demean the personal space of their victim's and weaken them.

Still, subtle manipulation will end up hurting in the end. These manipulators will attack their victims like silent little parasites and it slowly starts to corrupt their psychology. However, the victim has no clue about the manipulation that is happening to them. They realize what happened after the manipulator removes their self from their personal space, which leaves them feeling hurt.

A person's personal space is the stomping ground for manipulators. They are only able to hurt people if they learn their personal space and what is in it. This is why manipulators can read a person's identity.

If you were to question a manipulator about the personal space of others, you would get a response similar to "Space is only personal if a person lives in isolation. People show who they are through their actions and words, so how is that considered personal identity?" Manipulators will access every door that they possibly can.

- Self-protection

Every manipulator is trying to protect their self. In order to do this, they engage with others because they know how. Some manipulators don't have this skill. It is this sense of self-protection that drives people to manipulate others.

When a manipulator does something bad, self-protection becomes the reason behind it. As a result, manipulators don't ever question the actions they take. Everything is ultimately about their desires, motives, and feelings.

Self-protection is a natural human instinct, but most people don't use manipulation in order to protect their self. People who possess these manipulative abilities and have a strong need to self-protect breeds a dangerous personality. These types of people believe that their actions are needed, which is why they are great at rationalizing their actions.

Habits of Manipulator

It's hard to tell when a person is manipulative when you first meet them. But, there are little habits every manipulator possesses that you can keep an eye out for.

They play the blame game

They will constantly shift blame. They refuse to take responsibility for their actions. They will either lie if they have to or create some exit strategy. They don't have a code of ethics.

They minimize their actions

Everything that they say or do is "not a big deal." Ironically, they are typically the ones that make a big deal out of things. But, once they hear something that they don't like the sound of, they will turn the tables. They lack any empathy for people who have tried to help them and will willingly throw them under the bus.

They bully people

Manipulators are bullies. This doesn't include just insults. It can involve spreading rumors and alienation. They act very childishly. They will ignore certain people in group settings and try to keep them from voicing their opinion. This is their way of establishing dominance.

They insult people

They are, by nature, abrasive and rude. True friends often feel comfortable enough with each other to mess around and poke fun, but manipulative people go overboard with their insults. They will undermine others in social settings. They never grew out of that teenage mentality where it was cool to make fun of people.

They create guilt

Manipulators are great at making others feel guilty about something they didn't have anything to do with. There may be times when you don't have the energy to deal with something, and the manipulator will make you feel bad because you weren't there for them.

They share alternative facts

Manipulators will mold the truth to help them. They will hide certain information that they know is going to expose them for the liars they are. Manipulators approach interactions like they were in court because they believe everything they say can be used against them. They do this so that they have the ability to say, "I didn't say that," should the need arise.

They switch the subject

They will always steer the conversation toward things that they need. This is especially true when they know that they are the one in the wrong. Instead of proving the other person right, they will change the subject away from the current topic to avoid being found out.

They play dumb

Manipulative people will drain the energy out of the people they are around by looking towards them for help, and then they go ahead and do whatever they want. When they get called out, they will have an excuse at the ready. "It's my life, not yours." "I'll make my own mistakes." This is fine because it is their life, but they needn't start soliciting the advice of others if they aren't interested in hearing the truth.

They play innocent

Manipulators are great with playing with the truth so that they look like the victim. Your friend could constantly make you feel bad for not spotting them the money for cigarettes even though you hate smoking. They are simply trying to use you. They will try to make you out to be the bad friend and play all innocent if you were to ever say anything.

A manipulator could have hundreds of people in their life who love them, but they are a lone wolf in their mind. This lone wolf is cold-hearted and constantly on the hunt and nothing will stop them. Every situation they find their self in is a new chance to earn something. If they notice a person going through bad times, manipulators will get something from it. They start feeling excited if they notice bad things happening to others because they know that person is going to be vulnerable.

The manipulator lives in their mind. They are constantly plotting their next move. Life is just a game to them, which is why they never get tired. On the inside, they are rigid in their ways, while on the outside they act normal. The outward façade helps them to target others through their vulnerability.

Techniques for Effective Communication

You are at an advantage when you can communicate effectively. After all, you are the person who knows your goals and how you hope to achieve them. The point is that you are not going to achieve those goals single-handedly, because you don't live in isolation. Every single one of us needs allies, friends and supporters along the way. How do you work with other people unless you can get your point across? How can you develop strong and lasting allegiances unless you understand what's going on with the people you work with?

Earlier we discussed building influence and how you can achieve that through a variety of strategic devices, as well as being someone who models excellence in all you do. Now we'll look at some other techniques to support what we've already learned.

Following are some useful psychological techniques that help in effective communication:

Neuro-linguistic Programming (NLP)

Created in the 1970s by two California doctors (Drs. Bandler and Grinder), neuro-linguistic programming is a method employing theories of psychoanalysis and communication, toward helping people develop themselves more fully. NLP advances the idea that many of our behaviors are programmed and can be altered for the better, due to a link through linguistic and neurological realities. There are strong links between what we do, what we say and how we behave that Drs. Bandler and Grinder believed, in developing NLP, could be useful for the modification of undesirable or socially unviable behaviors. They further believed that these alterations would result in dramatic improvements in the quality of the relationships and professional lives of those who used these techniques.

NLP's goal is to understand how the human mind perceives things; how to use all your senses comprehensively to effectively send your intended message through verbal and non-verbal communication. NLP can also help you apply this understanding in order to communicate more effectively, by creating rapport between you and other people. Needless to say, how you present yourself and what you have to say matters a lot, with regard to the way others perceive you. When our neuro-linguistic patterning provokes behaviors that prevent effective communication, this can be "re-patterned" in order to deliver better results.

Does it mean you are failing if you can't persuade someone to change their mind, or budge on a dearly held position?

The answer is no. It just means you need a bit of personal tweaking. As we've discussed throughout this book, part of that has to do with understanding yourself and how you present to others. It also has to do with applying that knowledge to your own perceptions about other people. But when it comes to our behaviors (some of which have to do with non-verbal language), perhaps NLP is the silver bullet to more successful and fruitful interactions with other people. With your sharpened communication skills, you will still be fostering a constructive work environment, because NLP is helpful in doing that by virtue of the following characteristics:

- *Helps you communicate clearly.*

- *Helps you have a positive personal impact on people.*

- *Helps you build trust among colleagues and friends.*

- *Helps you put people at ease and by doing so, elicit sincere reactions and feedback from them.*

- *Helps you build respect among colleagues and friends.*

- *Helps you appreciate other people's point of view, even when it differs from your own.*

- *Helps you use the existing climate to bring about your preferred outcome.*

And what is the result of using the NLP technique?

- *Your workplace team can reiterate what you have communicated to them correctly and mirror your intentions, ensuring they deliver the outcomes you desire.*

- *You provide your team with the opportunity to express their opinions, even when they differ from your own. This tension is healthy and encourages creative dissent, which can build the team through confidence in your leadership and in the validity of team opinions.*

- *Your technique can enhance the impact of your verbal message, serving a complementary role. For example, a pat on the back, delivered in concert with a verbal message of approval for a job well done, has a reinforcing effect, which complements the spoken message.*

- *You can underline your verbal message, when you throw your hands in the air as you verbalize your exasperation. That is called "accenting".*

All of these changes in your communications style are possible with NLP. Of course, seeking out a trained professional to assist you with the process is highly recommended. If you feel that resorting to clinical help is necessary to help you succeed in life in places where you have gotten "stuck", it's well worth considering.

<u>Self-Hypnosis</u>

Just for clarification, this technique has nothing to do with the "Svengali effect", in which a stage hypnotist attempts to overwhelm your personal autonomy; inducing you to submit to his charismatic control. Life is not a movie. Here you are not going to learn how to put anyone in a trance.

This technique is concerned with fostering effective communication by encouraging your mind to work at a higher, level. You will learn to clear out distracting thoughts arising from your environment and to delve deeply into your thought processes. By following this technique, you can come to understand what you want and how you intend to go about getting it. You will also learn to decipher non-verbal cues you have noted in your interactions with others, providing you with an objective reading of all factors in any given situation. This process can enhance your objectivity and improve your ability to make rationally-informed and sound decisions.

In short, self-hypnosis helps you achieve the following:

- *Avoid distractions and improve concentration.*
- *Solve problems by having a better and more well-rounded understanding of them.*
- *Formulate ideas as part of a strategic plan you can then put into practice.*

Taking the time to train your mind to be quiet and to make space for rapid analysis and evaluation is a worthwhile pursuit. It may sound a little unorthodox, but making it possible for your brain to make decisions based on careful analysis, instead of being alive with detritus that's not serving you in the project of moving forward with your life is something which can genuinely make you more effective in every area of your life. Self-hypnosis can help you achieve this.

Identifying And Avoiding Manipulation

Manipulation is naturally very underhanded, and often, they key is for your own intentions to remain a secret. Because of this, it's difficult to understand when you are seeing such tactics unfold right in front of your face, or worse, when you've fallen victim to them yourself. Given that you're reading this book, it's safe to say that you may have already had a disturbing thought of uncertainty regarding this topic. Well, not every manipulation is going to look the same, however, there are red flags across the board that can assist you in identifying it.

Because manipulators make their moves in the dark, and hide their true intentions, they seldomly come straight to you with something that's on their mind. Instead, they'll dance around the subject, and take stabs at a situation from afar, usually causing confusion and anger. In other words, a common identifier of manipulation is when an individual is being passive aggressive. It's easy to tell that something is wrong because of the way someone is acting, but you're unsure of why they're upset, or if you've done anything wrong. This subconsciously tells the person being manipulated that they're in the wrong automatically. Not only for the original reason the manipulator may be upset, but also for not knowing the other was mad in the first place. The mature move would be to be honest about your feelings if you are indeed upset about a situation. This would allow everything to be out in the open, and everyone can begin working towards solutions. Those being passive aggressive don't necessarily want to reach a solution, they often want to be angry, and want it to be at the fault of anyone else.

Which also leads into our next point on identifying manipulation: your emotions mean less. In any situation where your own feelings are at stake, you will be made to feel as if the way you feel doesn't matter. If you announce that you're upset, then you're told you're overreacting to the situation. A manipulator is often dismissive of other people's emotions, especially if those emotions are a roadblock set on their own route. Not only will a manipulator attempt to downplay the feelings of others, they will also try insisting you're insane for being upset in the first place. People are made to feel as if they're going crazy, so the manipulator won't lose control of the situation.

Manipulators are constantly trying to get others to prove themselves. Nothing you've ever done is good enough, and not only do they let you know, but your heart is played upon so that you'll continue under their spell. This can be seen in many different relationship dynamics. In a platonic friendship, someone trying to manipulate their friends will be upset often. They'll insist that they've always been the better friend, and even question if they consider you a friend or not. The manipulator may even suggest you perform certain acts in order to prove your friendship is true. The same kind of identifier, but in a romantic relationship, would look like your significant other always telling you to prove you love them. No matter how many times you've said it, or shown it, you're always being asked if you truly love them. There's always something more to be done in order to prove your love.

At some point, there must be a breaking point. There will naturally be somewhere along the road that where a manipulator is told no. Of course, manipulators aren't going to take no for an answer, and this takes several forms. If you encounter a conversation where one person simply will not let up, then manipulation may be at hand. For instance, a classmate turns to you and asks if they can cheat off your final exam. Knowing your professor will fail anyone caught cheating, you tell your classmate that you'd rather not chance it. He continues, asking again, but this time adding on that he really needs your help. Again, you apologize, but just as before, you politely decline. This back and forth doesn't end there, but instead, ends when you feel so worn down that you give in.

A manipulator isn't going to stop until they get what they want from you, whatever that may be. Those in relationships could just as easily fall victim to these indicators, because they don't see anything wrong with someone continually asking. What's more is that you had already said no, and more than likely said no multiple times. As time goes on, it's more and more trying to say no to someone you care for, so each time it becomes more difficult. It's hard to identify this as it's happening, but a step back may give you the outside perspective needed to see the manipulation occurring.

Manipulators are often very kind people, but the difference is when you feel as if you're being killed with kindness.

Of course, not every kind person out there is going to have ulterior motives and honestly do things because they care. What you need to keep an eye out for is when the intentions for doing a good deed become skewed in a different direction. It's a little easier to catch it if you're looking at the situation through a window. For example, your boss buys his wife a nice diamond ring, and she's ecstatic. As she walks away with her next gift, your boss leans over to you, whispering that now his wife couldn't say anything got his new car next week. It may have been a nice original gift, but it was given with ulterior motives. You may think you've encountered a ridiculously kind person but try asking yourself what their true intentions might be.

It becomes tremendously more difficult when you're sitting on the other side. Usually, the only thing your boss' wife would see is the new diamond ring upon her finger. It's difficult to identify this tactic as it's happening, because the subject is generally unable to see past the initial kindness.

These acts of kindness can also be used to gain trust from others, but they always come with something else attached that favors the manipulator. Trust your instincts, above all. If you feel something is a little off, maybe you feel pressured in a strange situation, or you're starting to question yourself – then manipulation may be prevalent.

Above all, a lot of manipulators tend to be liars. However, it's easier said than done to go around knowing with absolute certainty that someone is lying, but at some point, you will realize you've fallen for their trap.

You're going to encounter all sorts of broken promises, missed dates, messy arguments, and conversations that are denied ever taking place. The goal is to gain power and control over others, and some people don't believe they can get that by being cunning, so they fabricate anything they can. These stories can make some sort of impression, build trust in some way, or to help them prove their own point. The most important part about being able to identify manipulation is to know who you're dealing with. Someone seeking to manipulate you is going to know you to some level of degree, does this person know what your triggers are, and would they use it against you? Knowing their favorite technique will always help you identify whether you're being manipulated and will further allow you to act upon that knowledge.

As stated before, remember that not all manipulation looks the same. Manipulation comes in all sorts of different boxes, but with our firmer grasp of understanding, and our guide to identifying it, I'm confident nobody reading this book will ever become a slave to it. Although, it is important to keep in mind that not everyone in the world is a manipulator. You're going to encounter these techniques out in the world without any ill will behind them, and that's a good thing. What a terrible thought to believe that every person you encounter could be seeking to influence you in a negative way. What's not a good thing, is categorizing each as manipulation anytime you encounter an odd feeling about a situation. Finding the middle ground between trust and distrust can be tricky, knowing where you fall on the spectrum is ultimately up to you. While these tricks can guide you when identifying manipulation, there are multiple other factors that play into it.

Now that we've learned tips and tricks of manipulation, as well as different forms it takes, how can we avoid it? Well, there's no pointer that's going to allow for a complete avoidance of manipulators. You can't know what kind of person someone is before you've even had a chance to meet them, but you can use helpful tools to assist in your navigation.

The thought of looking inward to discover the motivation of another may seem strange, but you just might find the answer. It could be that you allowed yourself to be manipulated because you enjoyed the attention. This could either mean you had a touch of loneliness, or it could involve something much deeper that may go back to childhood. It happens much more often, simply because everyone likes to be complimented. Who wouldn't take a compliment? However, try to catch yourself when you feel like you're being complimented too much. Better yet, if you're unsure of the intentions of another, be humble. You can thank them but may be explain that you don't honestly deserve so much praise. Another fast tactic is to direct the praise elsewhere. If you're being complimented on your dress, explain maybe you had borrowed it from someone whose style you enjoy. Maybe they do just want to compliment you, but these tips will guide you through this unknown territory.

The number one tip to avoiding manipulation you will hear is to get a thicker skin. Although this is a bit one-sided, it is true to some extent. To the truth, even ones who are stereotypically considered strong, physically or emotionally, can just as easy find themselves being manipulated. Those who are too kind, and are people pleasers, tend to be sought out the most by manipulators. Because of their trusting nature, they tend to fall victim more than any others, unfortunately. It's sad, but it's also reality. It's good to be open to the world around you, and accepting of others, but approach with a little more caution if you always find yourself getting the raw end of the deal with manipulators. Chances are you may be too trusting, and therefore an easy target for people looking to take advantage. This doesn't mean to close yourself off to the rest of the world. You shouldn't. However, this does mean to be more careful when meeting new people, because you never know who they really are until it's too late. Start a journal in which you write down your interactions with new people you meet and reflect at the end of the night. This will continually give perspective on how your interaction went, and how you are progressing with them. The purpose isn't to change who you are, but to make you more aware.

Know yourself. This can be difficult, because most of us are still trying to figure out who we are no matter how old we get. Know what you need to do to love and protect yourself. The hardest people to manipulate are the ones who love themselves and exude a certain confidence because of that.

A manipulator isn't going to try anything on someone holding their head high and has a strong sense of self. Practice self-love, and positive self-speak to avoid anyone getting the idea that they'll be able to take advantage of you. Strong-willed people aren't easily controlled, and this alone will fend off a good majority of manipulators.

One thing that this book has helped with that will help you avoid manipulation, is recognizing when it's occurring. Throughout this text you've learned all sorts of useful methods, and even how to identify manipulation. Being able to point it out is half the battle when it comes to manipulation, because nobody is going to like being found out. Not being able to hide is going to show their hand from the start. Remember, manipulation is all about guilt, blame, and shame. A manipulator will try to use any, or all these tactics. "I didn't do this because of you", "I have no one else", or simply doing things you don't want to, are all signs that you may be falling into a trap.

A good way to avoid manipulation, especially when you're being forced to deal with a manipulator is to keep the focus on them. Ask them probing questions, and get them to talk most of the time, instead of allowing them to gain knowledge about yourself. Naturally, the manipulator will want to come off as intriguing and interesting as possible and can rarely pass up an opportunity to talk about themselves. While some or most of these answers may be lies, that's not really the point. The point is to keep them from trying anything funny, or trying to one up you in any way. By keeping them speaking of their favorite topic, themselves, it stops them in their tracks when it comes to manipulation tactics.

The majority of this text has been speaking about kicking the manipulator to the curb, but it's also important to mention that it's not always ideal. Love and forgiveness do exist, and if you invite a manipulator to stay in your life, you'll need to set some major consequences. Above everything, you need this other person to know that you do not tolerate any sort of manipulative behavior. You may be kind enough to take them back into your life, but you are not kind enough to let it happen again. This will show the manipulator that the control center within your relationship has changed, and they'll need to follow your rules for the time being if they hope to earn your trust back. The way someone responds will also give your first glimpse if you're dealing with a changed person or not. As said throughout this book, manipulators love to be in control, it's what they strive for. Someone who isn't out to change isn't going to enjoy you being in control of the situation by setting consequences. It's possible they'll act out, or protest consequences, even try to spin it around on you as if you're being untrustworthy or crazy. This reaction will help you avoid any repeats in the future.

Don't allow someone to give you the silent treatment. This action can fall under a multitude of our types of manipulators, but above all else, it's childish. The individual is simply trying to get their way by not speaking at all, and refusing to speak to you unless you give in on something specific. As healthy adults, this is not the way to communicate with anyone. Giving into this childish behavior, is only teaching the other person that this is acceptable. Moreover, it's also teaching them that if anything doesn't go their way, they'll simply be able to repeat this behavior all over again for the same result of you giving in. This takes consequences to slightly different level in not allowing it to happen at all.

Remembering your rights will help you tremendously in avoiding manipulation. You are who you are, and above any self-evident rights within our governments, we also hold rights as human beings. You have the right to earn the respect of others. You have the right to your own feelings, and they are one hundred percent valid. You have the right to form your own opinions, and they do not have to be the same as anyone else's. You have the right to be happy, and that doesn't hinge upon the happiness of anyone else. You have the right to rank your own responsibilities and discover what is important to you. You have the right to make your own decisions and decide what is best for your wellbeing. You have the right to decline anything you want, and "no" means no.

Forgetting any of these rights, especially during times of trauma, opens us up to manipulators. Holding these true will not only protect you against manipulators, but it will also help you become a strong-willed individual. Lastly, avoid manipulative people whenever possible, and now that you have the knowledge, use it to help others. People you know and love and manipulated behind closed doors, or even in front of your eyes, all the time. Use the experience you've gained to aid you in the future. You know the signs and you know the warning, don't be the person that falls into the same trap time and time again.

68

The Difference Between Manipulation and Persuasion

Manipulation and persuasion are closely related. In fact, the two words are sometimes used interchangeably in casual conversations. Even in psychological literature, the line between the two concepts can blur at times. To truly understand the difference between these two concepts, we have to look at their dictionary definitions.

The simplest definition for the term persuasion is "the act of causing a person or a group of people to do something or to believe something."

Based on that definition, you can see that persuasion is something that is done every day, and it's fair to say that it's often done out of self-interest. When you persuade someone to change what they believe about something, the outcome is clearly meant to benefit whoever initiates the act of persuasion.

In as much as it's borne out of self-interest, persuasion is has a certain purity about it; it is not at all evil, and it is completely socially acceptable. In fact, it's a core part of social discourse; for example, leaders have to persuade people to vote for them.

Persuasion is not at all immoral, and even though it's often done out of self-interest, it's possible for someone to do it with altruistic intentions; for example, civil rights leaders persuade people to join their causes, not because it benefits them, but because it benefits other people.

Manipulation, on the other hand, is defined as "to change something by artful or unfair means in order to serve one's purposes."

In this case, the underlying self-interest is unquestionable. Even if the manipulative action you take is for someone else's own good, the bottom line is that it benefits you as well. The benefit that a third party or the target of the manipulation may gain in that case is a mere byproduct of, and the main goal is to benefit the manipulator.

Where manipulation is involved, there is a clear implication that the manipulator wants what he wants, no matter the consequences. That is why, unlike persuasion, manipulation makes use of techniques that are deceptive; the target is deliberately misinformed to increase his or her chances of making certain choices.

In general, psychologists agree that the difference between manipulation and persuasion comes down to 3 key things. The first thing is the intent of the person who instigates the persuasive or manipulative action. The second thing is transparency or the truthfulness that goes into the persuasion or manipulation process. The third thing is the net-benefit that results from the persuasive or manipulative action. In persuasion, the intent is generally constructive, while in manipulation, the intent is generally destructive. In persuasion, there is a lot of transparency and truthfulness, while in manipulation; there is a lot of deception and half-truths. In persuasion, the resultant action benefits all parties, but in manipulation, the resultant action benefits the manipulator a lot more than the target.

If someone describes you as manipulative, you will take it as a criticism. However, if he described you as persuasive, you will take it as a compliment. When you tell someone that you have been manipulated, in their mind, they'll register that information as a complaint. However, if you tell someone that you have been persuaded, they will think that you have arrived at a certain conclusion after objectively reviewing the evidence as it was presented to you.

Manipulation is thought to be immoral because it harms the person on the receiving end of the manipulative action. Sometimes manipulation can hide under the guise of persuasion, and that is when it is most harmful. Take the example of advertising. We tend to think of advertising as persuasion, or a fairly harmless form of social influence. However, when the company that creates the product hides crucial information from the customer, or if they lie about the benefits of their product in their advert, then that is manipulation.

For example, when big tobacco companies hid the harmful effects of tobacco from the public, or when they pushed back against scientific research in order to maintain the popularity of their products, that was manipulation, and not persuasion.

When advertising is based on truth and in scientific evidence, then that is persuasion. However, when it encourages people to form beliefs that are objectively untrue, that is manipulation.

Even when manipulation is used to help others, it still seems morally objectionable. For example, if you notice that your friend is in a toxic relationship, and then you manipulate her into breaking up with her partner, even if she is better for it, you will still feel like you have done something wrong. That brings us to an important difference between manipulation and persuasion; how the two concepts relate to free will.

In the example about, you may help your friend by manipulating her into breaking up with her toxic boyfriend, but in doing so; you have subverted her free will. When you manipulate someone, you technically make a choice for them, and they end up thinking that they made a choice by themselves. However, when you persuade someone, you present them with all the information they need to make the right choice. So, if you manipulate your friend into ending her relationship, even if the outcome benefits her, morally speaking, you end up having a lot in common with the toxic boyfriend you are trying to save her from. You are like a police officer who is willing to break the law in order to catch lawbreakers.

Now that you understand the difference between manipulation and persuasion, and you know the shortcomings of manipulation as an influence technique, should you continue using both manipulation and persuasion? Well, when it comes to persuasion, there is no objective reason why you should stop using it. However, where manipulation is concerned, you need to have an introspective debate with yourself and try to judge each situation on a case by case basis. Supposing you are a salesman and your livelihood depends on manipulation, will you stop using it? What if you are in a competitive workplace and the trajectory of your career depends on your ability to manipulate people; are you going to limit yourself to persuasion? Ultimately, it's up to you to decide what you can live with.

Take the Pressure Off

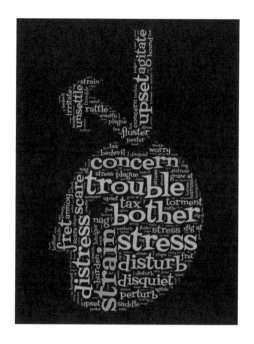

We all have days in which life seems to go wrong. We believe that we will not achieve our goals, the deadlines are upon us and, also, we feel we have no one on our side. It is effortless to fall into destructive practices when we are in those negative states, which puts us in a bottomless spiral downward in which we see things getting worse and worse.

Although it is indeed more comfortable to do things that lead to pessimism, it is also true that we have the possibility of reversing that tendency.

When we cannot dominate a situation, because uncontrollable factors come into play, we still have the chance to change ourselves.

How to better withstand the pressure

Take into account these essential tips that will help you fight pressure and improve your physical and mental state, a cycle very well related:

Take a breath

Do not be so hard on yourself. When we make a mistake or cannot finish a job on time, we often remember all the previous occasions when this has happened, and as a logical consequence, we despair. During a bad day, if you detect that you are judging yourself too hard, stop there, take a break and continue later.

Exercise

Although it seems strange to some, an excellent solution in the middle of a catastrophic day is to get up and run (or walk, if that is what your physical condition allows). If you can't get out, get up from the chair and do some stretching exercises while breathing deeply. Remember that your brain requires enough oxygen to function correctly and make the necessary connections. Provide for it.

Turn to your loved ones

If it is difficult for you to visit them at the moment, take the phone and communicate. Nothing better to ward off ghosts than human warmth. Don't underestimate the value of warm words from a family member or close friend. They work miracles.

Laugh with desire

When we spend difficult seasons, laughing becomes an arduous task. That is why we have to look for some source of fun that facilitates laughter. Although at these times we tend to watch a romantic movie or a drama that combines with our mood, it is best to see one of those light comedies that make us laugh by reflex. Follow this line, and you will feel lighter later.

Eat healthily

Yes, of course, eat healthy foods. Most of the time, when faced with an unusual amount of work or trying to finish a particularly tricky writing, we put together junk food to accompany us. This leads us to feel bad about ourselves, a result that is all counterproductive. However, if we can prepare a plate of raw vegetables or a colorful selection of seeds, our body will have extra energy of the best quality, and it will be easier for us to maintain a state of calm.

Pay attention to your breathing

Did you know that with fear, anger, despair, or worry, we stop breathing for moments? This is a physiological response that we can avoid if we remember to relax and breathe deeply and consciously, even in the most stressful situation. Again, the brain needs oxygen to order your universe. Do not deny it.

Achieve some goal

Sometimes all we need to feel our real value again is to have a small achievement during the day. For example, if, due to the overwhelmingness of an important task, you have forgotten the little things, stop and clean your room. Interestingly, the simple fact of having an orderly space and having achieved it despite the pressure will make you feel that you are capable of many other things and you will resume the rest with greater enthusiasm.

As you can see, there are several actions that we can take to mitigate the pressures we feel in the face of the commitments of daily life. The important thing is not to feel defeated, but to propose to comply with these details, which, although small, can significantly encourage us.

The Manipulative Boss

Let us now shift our focus from the general relationship with coworkers to the boss-subordinate relationship. How do you recognize a boss that is manipulative? Isn't the goal of every boss to get their subordinates to do as they want? Can we conclude that all bosses are manipulative in some ways?

Well, while it is true that every boss would like their subordinates to do as they want, it cannot be termed as manipulation because the outcome is always mutually beneficial to all involved – the subordinate, the boss, and the organization. It becomes manipulation when there is no benefit for the subordinate or when it is not a win-win situation.

Despite obvious red flags, a manipulative boss can keep employees working long and hard when they should have quit or at least raised an alarm. In this chapter, we shall look at various sneaky ways which a manipulative boss can keep employees focused on giving their best even when the work conditions are obviously bad.

Manipulative Tactics of Toxic Bosses

If you always feel drained and exhausted working for your boss, it may be a sign that they are toxic and are manipulating you. There is a huge difference between a tough boss and a toxic one. A tough boss is not necessarily toxic. Being a tough boss simply means being assertive in leadership style and holding others accountable for their actions and inactions. A tough boss can support, care for, and value their employees. They take the role of mentoring their employees very seriously and try to live by high standards.

A toxic boss, on the other hand, is an emotionally abusive bully who takes undue advantage of his or her position to influence others (and sometimes coerce them) into doing what they really don't want to.

A tough boss can gently nudge you and even push you to grow. He or she can help you in many healthy ways to overcome your weaknesses and improve on your strengths. But if you always feel that you are losing your self-confidence and self-esteem anytime you are with your boss; if you feel humiliated and unable to speak up, if your boss is always yelling at you, it means that you are not working with a tough boss but with an emotionally manipulative bully.

Here are some of the manipulative tactics bosses commonly use on their employees.

Reverse-Psychology Guilting

If you've heard your boss said, "*This is the best thing we can do for this company. But if you don't believe in this vision, you can leave,*" they don't really want you to leave. They are only trying to make you feel guilty for even contemplating to quit. This is an effective tool that managers use to rally support from employees, but manipulative bosses can also use it to keep you on a job that you really should not be doing. Con artists use this type of reverse-psychology to make you hang on in spite of your better judgment. It is like turning the tables around and making you believe that it's on you if you walk away. They are silently telling you to "*Walk away if you want, but know that we'll succeed with or without you. And if we don't, it's all on you."* Obviously, the average employee would not want to live with that type of guilt, so they'll stay even when they don't want to.

Covert Intimidation

If your boss is in the habit of reminding you of the "important" role they have played in your career and how helpful they have been to you in the past, it is a clear sign that they are taking undue advantage of your emotions. Equally, there could be implied threats such as *"if this isn't completed before noon, management may start laying off people, and you know how difficult it is to get a job out there."* All these are manipulative tactics that may be aimed at getting you to overwork yourself to please the boss.

"We Are In This Together"

While there is nothing wrong with organizing company rituals such as award nights, parties, and motivational talks to bring employees together and bond them to the mission and vision of the company, devious leaders can use that avenue to keep employees going. The human desire to belong to a group can be used by a manipulative boss to rally support. One of the biggest motivators for many people is the consensus. This is particularly true when people are not sure of themselves. They look unto to the behavior and actions of others and use that to determine their best course of action. In a work situation where almost everyone is in on the "team spirit", you either join the consensus or face stigmatization.

Us Against Them

A manipulative boss knows how to pit you against your competition in the office, against another rival company, or even against the world! They give you the impression that the job you are doing is so valuable it is why others are against you, but you can get ahead if you work even harder and be more committed to your job and to the boss. The line of thinking the boss wants to plant in your mind is that there is strength, power, and a lot more force in unity. So if you stick with the boss, you are more likely to succeed. In some cases, manipulative bosses will use terms that clearly draw the line like, *"you are either with me or you are against me."* Putting the employee on a spot that way is likely to force them to agree with the boss even if it is reluctantly.

Let's Change the World

Most good employees want to strongly believe that their little efforts are changing the world to be a better place. In fact, some employees would not mind taking a pay cut so long as their work is meaningful and has a positive impact on people. The problem is that manipulative bosses are aware of this and can cash in on this to make their employees work longer, harder, and even do unethical things. *"The end justifies the means,"* is a common line they use to confuse the mind of unsuspecting employees. *"How did you think other great companies changed the world? Sometimes you need to get your hands dirty!"*

What manipulative bosses do is to appeal to your sense of a "higher calling" and make you ignore the means and processes of achieving this so-called "lofty" goal. This is one of the sneakiest ways to persuade employees to ignore red flags. Manipulative bosses know that if they can strategically play on their subordinate's bias of a better world, it would be pretty easy to get them to overlook the due process of doing a thing and focus on the "bigger picture" because what they are doing is for the "greater good."

The Coerced Agreement

One clever way bosses manipulate their subordinates into agreeing with them is to end their remarks with a tricky phrase, *"don't you agree?"* Even though it sounds like a question or a possible invitation for further discussion, it really isn't. It is a trick to get the subordinate to either agree with the boss or be confrontational and disagree with them. The choice of being confrontational is always ignored because, in the boss-subordinate relationship, the boss has more power because of their position. Very few subordinates will like to be in disagreement with their boss even if it means agreeing reluctantly.

If a boss should ask, *"what do you think?"* then they give room to hear the candid opinion of the subordinate. But, *"don't you agree?"* is rather manipulative.

The Family Game

Be wary of bosses and leaders in the workplace who are quick to remind you that *"we are one big family in this place!"* More often than not, this is a tricky way to get you committed to their cause. Of course, you are not likely to snitch or blow the whistle on your boss even when they are involved in some unethical practice if truly your boss is part of your sweet family. Manipulative bosses like to take advantage of that family intimacy and sweet talk (and sometimes coerce) subordinates into doing things they shouldn't be doing.

Over Intellectualization

You may be an educated professional, but if you find yourself struggling to grasp the meaning of what your boss is saying, you may be battling with a boss who chooses to use his or her knowledge to intimidate and shame you. This is not the same as nudging you to learn more; rather, it is aimed at confusing you and making you waste valuable time trying to figure out your boss. It is another way to push the subordinate into submission.

Clever Escapism

Do you have a boss who seems to be in a hurry each time you bring up a work-related issue that needs to be addressed? Perhaps they are always trivializing or dodging the issue and trying to distract you or change the subject each time you raise them. This is a sign of escapism. They are avoiding challenging discussions and will eventually lay the blame on someone else, probably you!

Being Available 24/7

Working longer than you should is not healthy for you. However, a manipulative boss will feed you the, "*I need you to be available round the clock*", line after first praising your ingenuity to high heavens or after laying hands on some damning information about you. So, if you are being pushed to work longer than you signed up for, it is very likely that you are being taken advantage of by your boss.

"That's Your Problem"

When your boss tells you that an issue you brought before them is not their problem but yours, it can be quite demoralizing. Bosses who perceive their subordinates as threats perhaps because of their great work performance may adopt this manipulative method to demoralize them and stall their progress. This type of manipulation is targeted at discouraging the subordinate from bringing any issues or work-related challenges they have before their boss. With time, this will have a negative impact on their input, efficiency, performance, and productivity.

"That's the Way it's Done Here"

Another way a boss can manipulate a rising subordinate is to repress their growth by putting up a brick wall of resistance to change. When a boss says, "*We've always done it this way,*" they are clearly telling you that they are not open to change. It is either that they don't actually know how to improve existing rules or they think a change may make their positions vulnerable. It could also be that they don't want you to take credit for the change and will do all they can to squelch your attempt to suggest a new way of doing things around "their" organization. So, they a boss tells you *"that's the way it's done here,"* they are manipulating you into mindlessly following the status quo. It is like saying, *"don't make any waves here; just go with the flow."*

Breaking Free From A Manipulative Boss

Avoiding a manipulative person can be a lot easier if they are not your boss. How can you protect yourself from a manipulative boss without appearing rude, disobedient, and seen as being guilty of insubordination? Do you have to quit your job if your boss is manipulative? Knowing that your job might be your only means of livelihood and getting another satisfying job may be a stiff challenge, how do you deal with manipulation from your superior?

First of all, a manipulative boss is aware that you may be clinging to your job with every iota of strength, which is why they can easily capitalize on that and play you for a fool. So, the first thing you need to do is to consistently show that you are not a pushover. When your boss and other work colleagues can see clearly that you cannot be easily taken for granted, they will respect you.

Here are some practical things you can begin to do right now, to break free from a manipulative boss.

- Start working on developing your self-esteem. Read books on self-esteem, get a handful of self-esteem worksheets and begin to do the exercises to develop a positive self-image.

- Have a firm belief in your value, abilities, and expertise. This will make you have personal respect for yourself and improve your self-confidence. You know that you are very valuable to your organization so they wouldn't want to let you go easily.

- Learn how to be assertive in your communication. There is a huge difference between rudeness and assertiveness. You must have and show due respect to your bosses and superiors – that is a given. However, being assertive means calmly stating your own views without easily being dissuaded. Manipulative bosses don't have the patience to constantly argue their points. If they notice that you are always firm about your views (without necessarily being rude), they will leave you alone because they know you can easily spot their mind games.

- Respect your own boundaries. There is no point setting boundaries that you won't stick to. If you have a rule not to mix work with your family time, for example, don't allow your boss to push you into breaking this rule. Of course, there are exceptions to every rule and you will know when it is necessary to become flexible because it will be a one-off occurrence. But when it is a routine occurrence, then you are giving room for abuse of your boundaries. Be firm and polite when you turn down such requests and you do not have to offer any explanation.

- Improve your self-awareness so that you can be fully aware of your strengths and weaknesses. Do you believe people in authority easily? How easily do you allow praises to get to your head? How easily do you let criticism get to you? Are you always seeking to be in the good books of your boss? Take some time to really reflect on your thoughts and behavior at work. If you are being honest with yourself, this time of reflection will reveal a ton of information about your strengths and weaknesses which you may not have previously paid attention to.

- Be timely and prompt about your job delivery. Insist on professionalism in your relationship with your boss. Make sure that you are fair and reasonable in your dealings. If you maintain a professional relationship with your boss it will not be too easy for them to introduce manipulative habits when dealing with you.

- Don't let your boss use jargon and unclear directives with you. Ensure that you are very clear in your communication. Be firm and request concise directives and responses. Stick to requesting clear and concise directives even when your boss seems to sidestep your request with irrelevant talks. Sooner or later, he or she is bound to stop using the over-intellectualization tactics with you.

- If you have a boss or superior that tends to dodge issues or engages in any form of escapism, ask for a specific day or time when you can discuss work-related issues with him or her. Make sure to put your request in writing either through email or text messages as that can serve as your evidence should the need ever arise.

- In cases of extreme manipulative behaviors or in cases of serious unethical behaviors, do not be afraid to take the issue up with human resources. Manipulative bosses thrive because they feed on your fear.

- As a last resort, if all else fails, simply quit. It is better to quit your job than to be someone else's pawn for their dirty work.

CONCLUSION

Thank you for reading all this book!

Your wellbeing is intricately linked to your perception of the self. This perception is affected by your external environment (the people you interact with on a daily basis) as well as your internal environment (your dominant thoughts and feelings about who you are.) This is why it is a good idea to surround yourself with positive people and ideas that can sustain your inner positivity. If your external environment is constantly bombarded by negativity, there is a great chance for it to dampen whatever positivity that exists in your inner environment.

If there is one message, I would like to leave you with it is this: learn to silence the inner critic and all its negative chatter. To do this effectively, you must continue to feed your mind with the right kind of stuff.

You have already taken a step towards your improvement.

Best wishes!

CPSIA information can be obtained
at www.ICGtesting.com
Printed in the USA
LVHW050312290321
682793LV00020B/2028